Freud and Divination

BENT SØRENSEN

FREUD AND DIVINATION

*A pocket book on cards,
magic, and psychoanalysis*

ᒥ

EYECORNER PRESS

Freud and Divination: A pocket book on cards, magic, and psychoanalysis © Bent Sørensen 2021. Published by EyeCorner Press in the Pocket Book series. Design and typesetting by Camelia Elias. Image: *Deconstructed Freud* by Camelia Elias.

ISBN 978-87-92633-77-4
February 2021. Agger, Denmark

EYECORNERPRESS.COM

*All of the linguistic instruments of subtle
thought are dropped and abstract terms
are taken back to the concrete.*

– FREUD on Dreams
   (and, accidentally, also on Divination)

Contents

Introduction

Before I got promoted to my current job as Janitor at Aradia Academy, I was President of the PsyArt Foundation, an international scholarly body devoted to the study of Psychology and the Arts which organised an annual conference and published a peer-reviewed academic journal.

During my 30-year academic tenure I would sometimes encounter confused junior colleagues who couldn't fathom my approach to literature, so I taught myself to give people a label they could learn by heart so they could be more comfortable in their acceptance or rejection of my work. I started telling these people that I was a "Freudian Reader-Response Critic" – usually that shut them up, for a while at least.

But in a deeper sense I actually meant what I said. I read books, songs, art with a Freudian knowledge and compared the way they made me feel to the way they made others feel, and then I wrote about that. That was fun.

After I stopped doing that kind of academic work, I transferred the fun part to my work with cards (and magic). Same difference. Still fun. And that is what I wrote about in five so-called "Janitor's Corner installments" for a Special Edition of the Cards and Magic course we ran at Aradia Academy in 2020. This book is an edited version of those pieces.

What does Sigmund Freud have to do with magic and cartomancy, you might ask. Surprisingly much, I would say. In this Pocket book I am going to look at five key Freudian insights and apply them to the ways of and reasons for reading cards and performing magic.

The five insights can briefly be named as: The Death Drive; The Uncanny; De-negation; Dream Work; and Totem and Taboo. Along the way, student interaction (not always non-con-flictual) prompted me to write about a sixth area of Freudian and Post-Freudian theory, which I have now also incorporated in this little book – Narcissism as a social character.

Beyond the Pleasure Principle

W̶e begin with the most profound insight among these areas of Freud's thinking - that of the existence of something beyond the pleasure principle, namely what Freud nominated as the Death drive, or that type of activity that we knowingly or at least subconsciously are aware of will bring us displeasure or outright pain.

I am not talking about masochism here, although this is also an area of interest for Fortune-tellers who are very likely to get clients that usefully can be described as masochists. Many of us have already met such sitters who repeatedly ask the same question, knowing full-well that the answer will be the same as the last time they asked: "No, he doesn't still love you (in fact, he never thinks of you now, nor did he actually love you back then...)" The bit in parentheses is usually just muttered under the Fortune-teller's breath, in the interest of business.

Actually masochism is a psychological mechanism that is indirectly related to the Death drive, but it is more properly described as a psycho-sexual aberrance and I will not explore that further today. How else does the Death drive, or as some theorists call it, the Thanatos principle (in opposition to Eros, the Pleasure principle) manifest itself?

Freud inadvertently discovered the thing that lies "Beyond the Pleasure Principle" while observing his young grandchild. He was puzzled that the child found such obvious pleasure in hiding ("losing") its favorite toy, only to "rediscover" it immediately after with redoubled pleasure. So, Sigmund wondered, what is it that

13

doubles our simple pleasure of having and consuming our favorite thing, whether it's a toy, food, beer, sex, etc.? Why do we want to have (possess) our cake and eat it (lose it), too?

His answer was that there must be a drive as potent as our life force which had hitherto been little recognized but which leads people to risk losing all they have, only so they can regain it and consume the exact same thing they had all along, but now with redoubled pleasure. This is a paradox of the human psyche - that we desire enactments of our death as much as, or more than we desire life itself and all the drives that we associate with life - the drive to have sex, eat, procreate, generate wealth, art, and happiness.

So, if this is indeed a general human feature (at least among reasonably privileged middle-class Westerners on whom Freud based all his theories), that we gain pleasure from unpleasure on the expectation of unpleasure to cease and be replaced by the original pleasure, and by doing so we redouble our cathexis (the psychoanalytical term for allocation of emotional charge), then we should be prepared for that to show up when we read for clients.

They prepare themselves for the worst possible news, actually hoping to receive them, and for us as readers to add the all-important "But..." restoring the client to the path of the pleasure principle. We may think this feature is only a quirk of the thrill-seeker and adventure junkie, but no – it is a part of all human psyches, even that of your innocent grandchild!

I hope this can help elucidate some client responses and fears that might seem illogical and surprising, or even 'out of character'. Why would a person otherwise be so fearful and nervous before a reading that they can barely contain their excitement, or as Freud would call it, their "forepleasure"?

One way of testing this response pattern is of course to not provide the "But..."! Instead, if the reading brings The Tower, followed by

15

Arcanum XIII, don't "But..." the client back to safety and pleasure by suggesting that this means a 'great transformation' is coming. Simply say, "The cards suggest you'll meet a violent end very soon!"

The Uncanny

Next I turn my attention to the notion of The Uncanny. This is one of Freud's most interesting contributions for those of us who work with literary analysis, and the notions are easily applicable to cards and magic.

The term, "The Uncanny," comes from an essay Freud wrote in 1919, mainly on the tales of E.T.A. Hoffman. But since this of course was originally written in German, we need to go etymological for a little bit before entering into the contents of the article. The German title and main concept of the essay is "Das Unheimliche," which is most often rendered as "The

Uncanny" in English. But there are nuances gained and lost in translation.

In German, if something is *Unheimlich*, it is at once the opposite of homely (which can be taken to mean, 'at home with', and also 'cozy' and 'comfortable') and the opposite of secret. This is a grand paradox. How can something both be unfamiliar (and therefore uncomfortable or downright scary) and known (as in not hidden or secret)? Freud's explanation is that everything of that nature was once very well known to us, but then became repressed, only to most certainly return to us in a new form. This is what is referred to as the "return of the repressed." So, The Uncanny is a repertoire of things we were once terrified by, but learned to pack away in our subconscious, from which it will return to haunt us if the right trigger occurs. It is a list of our good, old secrets.

The English word 'uncanny' however has slightly different connotations than the German original. Uncanny means that which we are not 'canny' about. This word is now only a regionalism, but it goes back to Germanic roots in the words 'ken' and 'kenning,' which are the roots of the word 'know' in modern English. So, the Uncanny is that which is beyond our ken, but at the same time *genkendeligt* as we say in Danish for recognizable (I use the Danish word here to facilitate the realization that these words are related).

OK, that is the etymology. The Uncanny is that which brings back vague, frightful memories from just beyond our ken. What can those memories be memories of? Which events, objects, persons? A 'poetics' of The Uncanny can easily be extracted from Freud's essay, and a partial list could run like this: Fear of the loss of one's eyes; fear of being buried alive; uncertainty whether an inanimate object is alive or dead; fear of doubles, twins, and other uncanny resemblances; and fear of unlikely repetition...

As you can see, this list is very uneven, running from very specific fears that we likely have not all had as infants or young children, to quite general fears we all recognize. In the context of session 2 where we worked with omens and what in Norse mythology and Asa belief is called *jarteikn,* we can easily see how occurrences of uncanny events or phenomena would also be taken as omens or pointers to something significant and out of the ordinary, taking us out of our canny comfort zones.

Let me start with the general ones, and exemplify with a story.

Once I walked down a well-lit side street in the city I lived in. As I passed under a street light, the lamp went out. Strange, but obviously just a coincidence. I walked quite briskly on. As I passed under the next street light, it also went dark. Very strange and quite worrying. I looked around to see if anyone else was about, wondering if I was being pranked somehow. Seeing no-one, I walked on a bit faster, desiring to get home. By the time the third street light went out as I passed under it, I started running faster than ever before and since in my life. I made it home, of course, and to this day have no idea what happened that night. If it happens again, I'll most likely have a heart attack and die.

This story illustrates an important aspect of the uncanny. Exaggerated repetition. If I told it properly just now, you felt the anxiety in your gut that I also felt that night. That is the power of stories, to awaken the general human anxieties or other emotions we have, gratuitously and without trauma. Freud suggests that we manufacture these occurrences of repetitions as a result of a childish repetition compulsion, similar to the one he saw in his grandchild acquiring pleasure from repeatedly 'losing' and 'regaining' its toy (which made him formulate the Death drive we discussed above).

It is easy to see how an occurrence like this in cartomancy would trigger a similar experience: The sitter asks a question and Death appears in the middle of your three-card sequence. The reader laughs nervously, and explains that this was not a health reading, so Death means simply the end of something. The next string of three cards fall on the table, Death is the middle card. The sitter blanches. This WAS a health question. Irritated, the sitter insists: "Shuffle properly!" The reader apologizes, and shuffles vigorously for over two minutes. Three cards fall on the table - guess which card comes in the middle... The sitter runs away screaming.

Next up, fear of doubles, or things that are in two places at the same time. My favorite movie scene using this technique is from David Lynch's *Lost Highway,* where the protagonist meets a weird man at a party (played by Robert Blake), who engages him in conversation, saying "We've met before, haven't we?" The protagonist wants to know where that might be and the mystery man answers, "At your house. In fact I am there right now.". At which point this obviously disturbed man hands the protagonist his cell phone and asks him to call his own home number. He does, and the man he is talking to at the party answers the phone! He is clearly in two places at the same time, and one of them is where he definitely should not be — the protagonist's own sanctuary, his home...

In card readings, imagine that the deck you are dealing from suddenly has two identical cards in it. They both appear in a small reading you are doing for a do and don't situation, first in the "do"-position, then in the "don't". The sitter is angry and accuses you of cheating. You have no clue why suddenly there are two Tower cards in your Tarot de Marseille deck. The next day you hear your client was killed in a car crash on the way home from the consultation with you. Will you ever pick up a deck again?

To Freud, doubles are a remnant of a childish psycho-sexual fantasy of wishes unfulfilled, that potentially could be fulfilled if only we were more than 'one,' i.e. had 'doubles' like Robert Blake's character, which more than doubles his power by being more than one and being in more than one place at the same time.

So, what I urge you to do, is to step away from these horrific scenarios and analyze them. What are the cards telling us, if they keep popping in our spreads, or if there are odd doubles appearing in your readings all the time? Freud would no doubt suggest that there is something you are trying so hard to repress that you are making yourself fail. It wants to come out in the light and play. You may not recognize it for what it is, or what originally caused it to frighten you, but you will have to find out, if you want it to stop reappearing, or re-animating itself.

For example, the oddly specific fear of losing an eye or the ability to see, Freud refers back to the castration anxiety a young boy experienced when he went against his father's authority. The fear of being buried alive in actuality masks a desire to return to the safety of the womb. The uncertainty of what is alive and what is dead is related to infantile narcissism in which the child believes it is in complete control of the world (this can be observed in children's play with dolls, for instance), as it once was in its mother's womb.

If a similar primal fear is aroused in a sitter by an uncanny occurrence with the cards, be ready to address the underlying concern. In such a situation the reader has to become the analyst, and ask gentle questions, but most of all listen.

Intermezzo:
More on Uncanny Doubles

At this point in the course a student made an angry comment on Freud's lack of relevance to our present situation, because he didn't work with animistic and shamanic cultures. An interesting and a-historical comment, I thought. But as always the proof of the pudding is in the eating, isn't it? Can Freud deepen our understanding of cards that include representations of animals interacting with humans in a non-exploitative way, or cards suggesting a relationship between human minds and behaviors and nature?

Let's take a quick look at two such cards
from Sergio Toppi's *Tarocchi Universale* deck.
Of course Toppi, like all white males, is an
imperialist exploiter of aboriginal peoples and
a whitewasher and cultural appropriator of the
worst possible kind. He is also a colonialist and
indirectly an apologist for the slave trade, the
mass murder of indigenous populations, and a
general sexist asshole. Or maybe that's just me -
I don't know anymore. I like these cards though
- quite a lot, in my capacity as an almost dead
white patriarch oppressor, that is. [Possibly, this
whole paragraph should be read as sarcasm and
satire of 'woke' political correctness]

I have chosen Toppi's *Il Mago,* Trump 1, and
L'Eremita, Trump 9. A feature of all the Toppi
cards is the extreme focus on the human head
and face. He reduces the human figures in
the cards to a single component of their full
bodily presence. In literary studies we call this
a *synecdoche.* A part is made to stand for a whole,
simplifying its complexity in order to heighten

a point that one wishes to make. This means that the entire Magician-hood of Trump 1, must be expressed in the way his head and face is drawn and painted. And of course, the same can be said about the Hermit's head.

An advantage to this synecdoche is further that we get a larger view of the faces, so we can read expressions more clearly, which can be nice in contrast to the very stylized and cartoonish faces of the Tarot de Marseille.

However, Toppi balances out the exaggerated sized heads with another element in each of the cards. The Magician has a crow sitting on his head, or growing out of his head. Its full body is represented, rather than simply its head. It is held in the same color nuances as the magician's head gear, so they are to be seen as kin. We might say that Crow is Magician's familiar. Same phenomenon with the Hermit, whose hair is the top soil that a whole tree grows out of. The tree's roots become the disorderly strands of hair reaching across his forehead. In the tree is a bird, possibly another crow. The tree stands alone, as a Hermit of an arboreal kind.

Now we could also suggest that this is a hopelessly anthropocentric way of looking at these cards. Why not suggest that it is in fact Crow who is the Magician, and the head is just a convenient, statuesque object for it to perch on? This would be an eco-critical deconstruction of our anthropocentric gaze. Similarly then, the Hermit is really the tree, standing alone on a knoll with a buried statue underneath. I am straining your credulity a bit by these suggestions, and you might ask yourself where I am going with this.

Enter Freud: May we not suggest that the figures in these two cards are one another's doubles, and that their comparatively equal size suggests just such a reading. The cards have an upper figural element and a lower one of roughly the same size and importance. So the cards are balanced and suggest a state of equilibrium. No one element in the cards is complete or can stand or be read in isolation. They are each other's doubles, but uncannily we cannot tell exactly where one figure stops and the other starts.

This is particularly clear in the Hermit, where the face melts away and everything, pictorially speaking, tends downward. With the Magician, the elements are more in parallel - his nose, the crow's beak; his headgear, the crow's plumage; his facial lines, wrinkles or tattoos, the crow's ruffled feathers.

Where does the human stop and the natural, non-human begin? That is the wrong question, Freud would teach us. We are the ones who try to humanize the 'wild' in these cards, but we could just as well try to do the opposite, as I did in the above deconstruction. The only pure human thing in these cards is the illusion of our humanity we have when we look at them. The wild is our repressed ego-content, that we have attempted to store away in the basement of the Id. The 'Call of the Wild' is only a call that echoes within our psyche. The 'wild' is always already with us, part of us, all of us.

De-negation

This chapter is about a very short article Freud wrote in 1925. As much of his best work, this article draws on observations from his clinical practice, which he then tries to elevate to a more general theoretical insight. He did this early on with the Interpretation of Dreams, as well, for instance, which I'll return to in the next chapter. This inductive approach is both a great strength in Freud's work, and at the same time the greatest point of weakness for his critics, who always criticise the value of his samples which admittedly are limited in terms of class, race and gender representation.

In the article I am referring to, the topic is the idea of what Freud in his native German called *Verneinigung*. In Danish we would call it *Benægtelse*, but in English it is hard to get a very good rendition of the word and phenomenon. The essay has been translated as *Negation*, pure and simple, but this is in fact an oversimplification. Therefore I suggest in line with the philosopher, Jacques Derrida and an academic friend of mine, the historian of religion and philosophy, Mark C. Taylor, that we dub the phenomenon *De-negation* instead.

You'll see why this is so in a minute, but let me start with reproducing Freud's clinical example of the phenomenon, which clarifies everything. Freud writes:

"Or: 'You ask who this person in the dream can be. It's *not* my mother.' We emend this to: 'So it *is* his mother.' In our interpretation, we take the liberty of disregarding the negation and of picking out the subject-matter alone of the association. It is as though the patient had

33

said: 'It's true that my mother came into my mind as I thought of this person, but I don't feel inclined to let the association count'" (S. Freud, Standard Edition, 1925, vol. 19, p. 235).

So, the phenomenon – or actually now we can allow ourselves to call it a 'technique' - is to take the client's negation out of the sentence uttered, and disregard, or denegate it. In other words, the client negates (a fact) and we denegate the client's action (which is caused by the urge to repress an unpleasant psychic energy) by removing the client's negation from the utterance. You can now see that it is wrong to call Freud's essay *Negation,* since that would make it be about what the client does, rather than about what the analyst does.

Now, it is important to set up some limitations to when this act of de-negation is permissible for the analyst. We cannot go around de-negating every sentence ever uttered, now can we? What Freud suggests, but not in so many words, is that the analyst can perform the act of de-negation when the utterance already reveals too much. In the example with the client's dream, it is clear that the remark that it was not the client's mother is unwarranted. Unprompted by the analyst, as well. It is an extra piece of info that 'slips' out of the client's mouth. In fact, this is what Freud felt happened all the time in various types of speech, for instance all dream recounts, but also in jokes and normal miscues in speech – the notorious "Freudian slips."

If a client is prompted directly and answers in the negative, we are duty bound to take their word at face-value, at least temporarily, but if the client volunteers info, we can denegate it at any time, esp. if we have prior knowledge that there is psychic energy contained in the topic being referred to by the client. Mothers and fathers are prime candidates for being such subject matter, of course, since it is in childhood that most of the troublesome, un-cathected energies are created.

Now, you can no doubt already see the use of this in cartomancy. When we substitute the terms reader and sitter for those of analyst and client, we can almost do a one-on-one correlation. How often have we not as readers felt that the sitter was less than 100 percent honest with us about what their question is caused by or actually refers to? And if we pull a card and ask the sitter to contemplate who he thinks the person in the card represents, how often have we not heard words to the exact same effect as Freud's client's "It's not my Mother?"

The next time you talk to a client try asking them who The Star is to them, or the Emperor. If they answer in the negative: "My Father was not like that, and I always respected him for it!" denegate that answer and take it – gently – from there. Likewise, if the sitter says: "But I don't love her!" Or, "I never cheated on my wife, never doctored the books, never stole a candy bar, never wished my boss would die," etc. etc.

This may sound like a cruel and cynical approach to psychotherapy or card reading, but we should remember what Freud says further about the cause of the client's negations. For Freud, negation was actually the first step towards bringing back repressed content into the consciousness of the client. That which cannot be spoken outright, can first be mentioned by being negated. By denegating it for the client/sitter we help them realize that it was repressed to their detriment, and that bringing it out will release the traumatic content for them.

At first, we should expect that the client/sitter will negate our suggestion that something is in fact so (the opposite of what they propose), and their reaction will be 'I didn't mean that, or "I didn't (ever) think of that.' We now know what to do with such negative sentences.

Freud concludes his essay with the words that "in analysis we never discover a 'no' in the unconscious, [nor that] recognition of the unconscious on the part of the ego is expressed in a negative formula" (ibid, p. 239). Therefore we keep going until the negations disappear without us having to perform the de-negation process, and then, and only then, can we truly help the sitter.

The Interpretation of Dreams

I now take a look at the notions of dream work and the interpretation of dreams — which according to Freud has to do with direct transmissions of repressed material from our psychological history that occasionally bubbles up to the subconscious, where dreams help it acquire a language which the patient can access in dream recounts — and with the help of the analyst come to understand with their conscious mind.

The other night my partner Camelia had a strange dream. She was working on some course material and a person in the course

Facebook group said something she couldn't quite hear but took to be a critique of her feedback to his posts. She protested and said that she was doing all she could. The person quickly exclaimed, "Oh, no – I didn't say anything about the feedback at all! I was looking for something to buy..."

The person had a strange name in the dream which Camelia described as Liocell, or something like that. The way she pronounced it to me immediately made me associate it to the Danish words "Lej og Sælg," which translate as "For Rent or Sale." Camelia's subconscious was making her brain mix things up that were only circumstantially connected: Facebook Marketplace where some friends of ours were selling a lot of strange items, and the Cards & Magic Course Facebook group where she had been stressing to comment on as many posts as she thought she should.

Her subconscious made her a gift of Mr. Liocell, the unhappy customer, who instantly blanched and retreated when she flashed her Samurai sword at him.

Freud claims that all dreams the client is able to remember have two levels, a manifest one and a latent one. In the manifest level the client accounts for what she remembers of the dream. This is where the contact point to the day's events also appears. In Camelia's dream she had been working on feedback immediately before bed, and this manifested itself in the dream. The latent level is where the subconscious twists the realities around to make a point to the conscious mind, but to such an extent that the client will often not be able to make heads or tails of it. Camelia was irritated that our friends were leaving town and selling their junk, and she was also irritated at having to work late on feedback.

Her subconscious created a focal point for her anger in the form of Mr. Liocell, and she quickly subdued him with this very anger. This part of the dream, Freud argues, is usually a representation of a wish fulfillment fantasy. In Camelia's dream, Mr. Liocell was clearly lying (as his name also indicates) about his desire, once she bit back at him. Her wish was obviously to subdue any criticism of the course, before it even got voiced.

In dreams, more than one event and several agents in a situation are often condensed into one situation/person and events are temporally displaced, just as geographies are spatially displaced. This is why dream logic is magical – time and place are out of joint, and characters we don't know that we know may appear. Camelia never met Mr. Liocell, and he is not real - and yet he may be a composite of our friends moving and several students in this class. He was able to speak to Camelia, and she to him, on Facebook - without using the chat, and simply through the comments and posts, which had suddenly become audio-visual, making it easier for her to scold him. Wish fulfilment, mixed with anxieties: what if Facebook actually hears everything we say? Can they hear my comments when I listen to a live Facebook video, etc. etc.

Now, for the dream to become valuable for the client, it has to be interpreted. Here we again need to look at etymology. Freud's book is titled, in German, *Die Traumdeutung*. It is not wrong to translate *Deutung* as interpretation, but that word in German would much more normally be *Interpretation,* or even *Auslegung*.

The German word *Deutung* in fact means something else. In Danish we say *tydning*. These words are found in two registers only. One is literary analysis, where they refer to uncovering obscure allusions and references, or even deciphering the author's very (hand)writing itself. And the other is fortune-telling and divination.

In divination we read manifest signs and correlate to another realm, namely the one we make inquiries about. In *Deutung* there is no one-to-one correlation between sign and meaning. There is always something obscure about the signs, and they require a 'reading' of them to become clear.

So, Freud deliberately used the word *Deutung* and not any of the other available ones, because he needed to convey already in his title the notion of the two layers, levels, and systems: The manifest, which needs a reader to become clarified into an interpretation of the latent content.

This is the strongest correlation in all of Freud's works between what he did as an analyst and what we do as readers of fortunes, or cards, or omens, etc. We are all in the business of *Deutung*. When we ask our sitters to comment on cards in front of them we prompt a recount in the same vein as a dream retelling. The manifest content is not from dreams, but from visions provoked by the images on the cards. The latent content is up to us as readers to guide the sitter towards.

We can use de-negation, free association and other well-known psychoanalytical repertoire to the extent we feel like it, or re-invent the wheel as intuitive readers if we prefer. As you already know, I like to be a little Freudian in my approach.

It is no coincidence that it was also in the field of dream study that Freud went all out and suggested something supra-personal was going on. He came to believe that some dream content was telepathically transmitted from person to person. Some card readers believe the same thing happens via the medium of Tarot cards between readers and sitters.

This part of Freud's writing was largely suppressed by his followers who worried that supernatural beliefs were detrimental to the scientific status of psychoanalysis and by implication to their earning ability.

Jung went all in on the supra-personal level with his ideas of archetypes, serendipitous synchronicities and all that jazz - and that is why his work has generally been seen as more conducive to our line of interpretative business.

But I believe we are all in the line of *Deutung* and can also learn from Freud in that business.

Totem and Taboo

I n the final chapter originally planned for this little book, I turn to one of Freud's most discredited works, *Totem and Taboo* from 1913. In this work Freud attempted to be an anthropologist without doing actual field-work, and to combine psychology and cultural studies, as it were. The problem was that he was mired in notions of primitivity with regards to native, non-European cultures and therefore saw analogies between childhood psychological structures he had observed in Europeans and native cultural patterns that he perceived as infantile. This of course is a settler/colonizer and potentially racist approach to other cultures that we cannot condone in any way.

But as practicing magicians we are inherently interested in practices across cultures that are designed to bring humans in deep contact with other beings, whether spiritual ones such as ancestors, physical objects with special properties, or animals which have different sensory perceptions of the world compared to us. In other words we are interested in Totems and why certain ways of interacting with humans, animals and objects may be so dangerous for the existing order that they are declared Taboo.

I propose two engagements with this topic: 1) Looking at Freud's text anew, to see what might be redeemed for our purposes. 2) Looking etymologically at the two concepts, Totem and Taboo, to see where that might lead us in terms of syncretism.

Freud looked at Australian aborigines to investigate their system of totem animals. He postulated that the true reason why the system was in place was as a marker of family structures, so that incest between close relatives was easily avoided. Instead of the European bourgeois family as unit, the aboriginal system works with the clan as its unit, and clans are defined according to the totemic emblem of each clan.

Clan management in this culture and several others in the Pacific and in Africa work through avoidance and isolation. In other words it is Taboo to marry or even socialize intimately between brothers and sisters, fathers and daughters, children and in-laws (as we would call them) within your own clan.

Freud further suggests that Taboos are naturally reinforced because we generally feel uneasy around other human beings, and therefore it is easy to amplify this neurotic behavioral pattern into a general rule of Taboo. If this unease with strangers becomes a pathology we have what Freud called a neurosis, and he suggested that cultures that enforce strong Taboos inadvertently also further a neurotic personality in the clan members. Now we are getting to something interesting, because this neurosis is due to the phenomenon of projection.

We feel uneasy around others, because we are insecure of ourselves. This we do not want to admit, and therefore we project the cause of the symptom onto others. I personally believe this is the mechanism we so rampantly see unfolding now in racist manifestations. We in the dominant white cultures in the West see that something is not right about the way we conduct ourselves vis-a-vis nature, the climate, our production and consumption patterns, our military spending, etc. This unease with ourselves is then projected onto the Other, very often a racial Other, who gets blamed for forcing us to react the way we do. We create a racial Taboo, in other words.

Freud also has an explanation for the choice of Totem and the animistic belief attached to them. He suggests that we create animist totems because we need to cultivate and justify our desire for control (ultimately omnipotence), and this we do by creating supernaturally powerful Totems. He situates this back to the phase where the infant is narcissistic and also connects it to later personality disorders such as obsession, delusion and phobias. We project the feeling of omnipotence away from ourselves and onto power objects and animals that we then pretend have those supernatural abilities. Freud saw this as specific to so-called 'primitive' cultures; I see it as what happens in our Western cultures with organized religion and cults of various kinds, including political ones.

Let's leave Freud for a minute now and look at etymologies. Totem is in fact a word borrowed from the Ojibwe language, which settlers came into contact with in the 17th century - first French-speaking colonisers of America, later English-speaking ones. In Ojibwe the collocation the whites most likely heard was *nindoodem,* my clan, my totem, my village *(oodena)*. So, totem literally means dwelling together.

We note that the segregation aspect Freud made much of in his discourse on Australian aborigines is absent from the etymology of the Ojibwe word.

Taboo on the other hand is a Polynesian language group word, found in many different variants from Hawaii *(kapu)* to Fiji, Vanuatu to Papua New Guinea. Settlers first came into contact with the word and concept in 1777 when Captain Cook learned about it on Tonga and it traveled back to Britain. The original form is likely to have been *tapu*, and it was misheard by the settlers. Its core meaning in Melanesian cultures was something elevated and therefore set aside for its value. Only by derivation does it mean something forbidden, because that is the ritualistic consequence of an object being sacred: not everyone is allowed to handle it because they won't know how to properly do so.

Both the key concepts are then native in or-igin, and were adapted by European settlers to

mean something slightly different and culturally skewed to their Christian, euro-centric world
view. This also means that we must redeem
the terms from Freud's embedding them in
his psychoanalytic vocabulary. Totems are not
primarily designed as a protection against incest
as he suggested – they are markers of kinship
inclusion instead. Taboos are not projections of
neurotic symptoms created to protect a fragile
ego formation – they are markers of sacred
distinction and worship instead.

So, what can we redeem, if anything, from
Freud's *Totem and Taboo?* We should make
good note of the notion of projection, for one.
Freud is guilty of projection himself in this
line of thinking, in that he suggests that similar
psychological mechanisms to those that rule
European middle-class infants, would also
completely circumscribe cultural practices in
clan-structured non-European cultures. That
is a fallacy. There may well be incest-protec-
tion customs in place in those cultures – after

all cultures that don't have such are less likely
to make it for centuries due to hereditary and
genetic repercussions. But the rituals of Totems
and Taboos are there to remind the members of
those cultures that they are not at the center of
the universe and certainly not alone as rulers of
nature.

I'd suggest we try to learn from that instead.
We should be aware of the mechanism of projection and apply it to ourselves and our own
culture. So, when we perform magic and enlist
help from familiars, for instance, we should not
assume a master-servant relationship between
us and them, nor should we perform magic to
enforce our cultural settler relationship with
the world.

What can the cards tell us about this? I suggest we read the Tarot Major Arcana as a story
about this relationship with the surrounding
world. It is a didactic, albeit Christianized,
allegory about our place in the greater scheme
of things. At the bottom rank are the earthly

instrumentals of rulers and religious function-
aries. We need to get past Arcanum XII and
XIII before things get really interesting. That is
where we meet the figures that are totemic and
teach us the deeper meaning of Taboo.

Temperance and the Celestials are particularly numenous and instructive of this, but
we should also learn from those that teach of
obsessions (XV) and cataclysms of belief (XVI).
I base this on my understanding of the Tarot de
Marseille, of course - but many green, Pagan,
Wiccan, Aquarian, etc. decks have similar
teaching potential. It's there for us to see and
hear, when we open our eyes and ears to *nindoodem and tapu.*

Afterword – On Narcissism

Freud was indeed bound by his time, gender, class and race, as I have pointed out in the above. There was no escaping this at that point in the history of the patriarchy, so we should expect his work to have limitations, and we should of course call them out when they create issues for our current use of his theories. I don't intend to sanitize the ugly bits in Freud, but I am 1) condensing his arguments, and 2) focusing narrowly on what we can still use of his ideas in a cards and magic context.

So, when a student said about the idea of narcissism being behind the uncanny effect of blurred distinctions between animate and inanimate that Freud's claim was "utterly wrong, and reeks of colonialist whitewashing" I was not completely in disagreement.

I tried this argument: it is correct that Freud is not thinking in pre-Judeo-Christian, animist terms at all. He couldn't; having based his observations almost exclusively on white, upper middle-class Viennese patients, predominantly married female ones to boot. He did have a strong interest in other cultures, but this interest took a largely objectified form, except in rare cases such as when he wrote *Totem and Taboo* in 1913. He collected artefacts from other cultures to the point of obsession throughout his life, but did not really attempt anthropological field-work.

I also agree that we should think in wider cultural terms than Freud was able to, and we do find strong inspiration from animist traditions in our magical practice. However, that has nothing to do with narcissism whatsoever, so the point is being a bit muddled by these conflations. Regardless of what cultures we are talking about, there is an element of child rearing present, which among other things involves teaching children what they can and cannot do. That also includes a child's unavoidable feeling of omnipotence, inspired by the child's supreme rule over its mother's womb. Once born, the child must realize that it is not in control of everything, and for instance does not have a monopoly over the mother's breast, nor the ability to kill and reanimate at a whim.

So, while objects can be and are animated regularly in the real world, especially among indigenous peoples, they are not so done by infants. Such skills come later in life, and not for everyone in the core shamanistic or animistic cultures.

The student's argument was, it turned out, chiefly intended as an argument against Freud's notion that infants all go through a necessary developmental phase which he dubbed primary narcissism. Again the claim was that this is only true for Western cultures under industrialism, and that Freud was being a universalist, or nativist theoretician claiming a cultural phenomenon as an innate one. In fact, I agree that Freud has such tendencies, and narcissism is much better regarded as a culturally specific feature when we look at it as a disorder.

Narcissism, however, is very real in the cultures of the Western world, and in the generation now reaching the level of tertiary socialization (and the one previous to it), it has become a major societal issue in the whole post-industrial world, so we need to understand it.

Let's look at what narcissism really is all about – in Freud and in later socio-psychological applications and extrapolations. For Freud, narcissism was a natural phase every child must pass through in its development, so there is nothing stigmatic about infantile or primary narcissism. In this phase the child's ego is constituted, and the superego is partially installed to regulate the child's behavior and keep it safe.

Narcissism is a necessary experiment for the child, as is the response of others to its behavior.

For Freud's student, Lacan, this evolution started in the mirror stage, where the child realizes for the first time that it is a separate entity with a body that is no longer attached to its mother. That is a crucial insight for the child's survival, and painful as it might be, it is necessary to get through.

So, it's only when the child fails to evolve out of primary narcissism and remains with a narcissistic injury that things become problematic. This typically occurs when parental and broader social correction of the child's selfish behavior doesn't occur in the right measure. Such children may remain in a secondary phase of narcissism and have their ego limitations insufficiently established.

Boom – Donald Trump. Boom – Patrick Bateman. Given to outbursts of rage, compulsive lying for purposes of self-aggrandizement, and abrupt descents into self-loathing and poor self-care, and ultimately displays of gratuitous violence. I realize that one of these two figures is slightly more fictional than the other, but their utterances can be analyzed with the same techniques anyway.

Christopher Lasch and other social-psychologists, already in the late 1970s and 1980s, postulated that narcissism had been installed as a social character by permissive parents who, however well-meaning, did their kids a disservice by allowing them to do things that reinforced them on the scale of omnipotence. Temper tantrums became tolerated, and the children in their quest for instant gratification took over the households.

That generation of narcissists have now grown up and have had kids of their own, who of course show even poorer superego management, since their parents have been unable to guide them. We are now seeing a third generation reach their twenties, who have had narcissistic parents and grandparents. Their grandparents were late Boomers and early GenX'ers, if you insist on applying the American generational sequencing. Their parents were Generation X or Y, and the current bunch are of course Millennials. All those terms are US-centric and more interesting for cultural analysis than for psychological understanding, so let's put them aside.

The latest generation includes those who have inflated senses of entitlement, and who resist being challenged in the educational system, preferring instead being catered to and spoon-fed pablum. They find it hard to think for themselves, and fail to understand why they suffer from mood swings and depressive states of mind. Many are also afflicted by attention deficiency tendencies and learning disabilities, and yet they are expected to go through secondary and even tertiary educational programs. But I digress, and should leave my professional woes as an academic of over 30 years of university experience aside. Let's instead consider what this may have of effects on a cartomancer's practice.

If we encounter a narcissistic sitter - and we will, because our profession attracts people who like to be the centre of attention – what should we do to force them to see that other people have agency over their lives in areas and ways that trigger them? One thing we can offer is a story where the sitter is not the absolute protagonist. Not every card in the deck is you. Some may represent your father and mother, teachers and love interests, too. And – horror of horrors – sometimes you, dear entitled sitter, do not appear in the spread at all.

It is not the end of the world, or your ego when that happens. Instead, sit back and enjoy the stories told by the cards, even if you are not in them. That way you may learn to mirror yourself in other figures, rather than just your own reflection. That way creatives may be able to help you see more clearly, and maybe even Freud can assist in polishing that mirror.

www.ingramcontent.com/pod-product-compliance
Lightning Source LLC
Chambersburg PA
CBHW010728270326
41930CB00016B/3413